Luck

Langston Hughes

(1902-1967)

Sometimes a crumb falls
From the tables of joy,
Sometimes a bone
Is flung.

To some people
Love is given,
To others
Only heaven.

Poetry In Motion© 1996 Marlowe, New York

New York City Transit
In cooperation with Poetry Society of America

Riding on a Railroad Train

EXCERPT

Oh, some like trips in luxury ships,
And some in gasoline wagons,
And others swear by the upper air
And the wings of flying dragons.
Let each make haste to indulge his taste,
Be it beer, champagne, or cider;
My private joy, both man and boy,
Is being a railroad rider.

OGDEN NASH (1902-1971)

Poetry In Motion© 1996 Marlowe, New York

New York City Transit
In cooperation with Poetry Society of America

WESTERN WIND

Anon (BEFORE 1500)

Western wind when wilt thou blow
the small rain down can rain
Christ if my love were in my arms
and I in my bed again

Our thanks to Poems on the Underground.

⊖ Poems on the Underground

Reprinted from *Poems on the Underground* (Cassell 1992)
Manuscript reproduced by permission of The British Library Board

Poetry In Motion© 1996 Marlowe, New York

New York City Transit
In cooperation with Poetry Society of America

POETRY IN MOTION

You say, "I will come."
And you do not come.
Now you say, "I will not come."
So I shall expect you.
Have I learned to understand you?

Komu to yū mo
Konu toki aru wo
Koji to yū wo
Komu to wa mataji
Koji to yū mono wo

Lady Ōtomo no Sakanoe (8th century)
Translated from the Japanese by Kenneth Rexroth

Poetry In Motion© 1996 Marlowe, New York

New York City Transit

In cooperation with Poetry Society of America

love is a place   yes is a world
& through this place of   & in this world of
love move   yes live
(with brightness of peace)   (skilfully curled)
all places   all worlds

E.E. Cummings (1894-1962)

Poetry In Motion© 1996 Marlowe, New York

New York City Transit
In cooperation with Poetry Society of America

POETRY IN MOTION

UNFORTUNATE COINCIDENCE

By the time you swear you're his,
*   Shivering and sighing,*
And he vows his passion is
*   Infinite, undying —*
Lady, make a note of this:
*   One of you is lying.*

—Dorothy Parker (1893-1967)

Poetry In Motion® 1996 Marlowe, New York

New York City Transit
In cooperation with Poetry Society of America

Aspects of Eve

Linda Pastan (b. 1932)

To have been one
of many ribs
and to be chosen.

To grow into something
quite different
knocking finally
as a bone knocks
on the closed gates of the garden—
which unexpectedly
open.

Poetry In Motion© 1996 Marlowe, New York

New York City Transit
In cooperation with Poetry Society of America

Blackberry Eating

I love to go out in late September
among the fat, overripe, icy, black blackberries
to eat blackberries for breakfast,
the stalks very prickly, a penalty
they earn for knowing the black art
of blackberry-making; and as I stand among them
lifting the stalks to my mouth, the ripest berries
fall almost unbidden to my tongue,
as words sometimes do, certain peculiar words
like *strengths* or *squinched*,
many-lettered, one-syllabled lumps,
which I squeeze, squinch open, and splurge well
in the silent, startled, icy, black language
of blackberry-eating in late September.

Galway Kinnell (b.1927)

Poetry In Motion© 1996 Marlowe, New York

New York City Transit
In cooperation with Poetry Society of America

Magic Words

Translated from the Inuit (Eskimo)
by Edward Field

In the very earliest time,
when both people and animals lived on earth,
a person could become an animal if he wanted to
and an animal could become a human being.

Sometimes they were people
and sometimes animals
and there was no difference.

All spoke the same language.
That was the time when words were like magic.

The human mind had mysterious powers.

A word spoken by chance
might have strange consequences.

It would suddenly come alive
and what people wanted to happen could happen—
all you had to do was say it.

Nobody could explain this:
That's the way it was.

Poetry In Motion© 1996 Marlowe, New York

MTA New York City Transit
In cooperation with Poetry Society of America

Delta

Adrienne Rich (b. 1929)

If you have taken this rubble for my past
raking through for fragments you could sell
know that I long ago moved on
deeper into the heart of the matter

If you think you can grasp me, think again:
my story flows in more than one direction
a delta springing from the river bed
with its five fingers spread

Poetry In Motion© 1996 Marlowe, New York

New York City Transit
In cooperation with Poetry Society of America

FROM
Ode to the Cat

Pablo Neruda (1904-1973)
Translated from the Spanish
by Ken Krabbenhoft
Illustration by Ferris Cook

There was something wrong
with the animals:
their tails were too long, and they had
unfortunate heads.
Then they started coming together,
little by little
fitting together to make a landscape,
developing birthmarks, grace, pep.
But the cat,
only the cat
turned out finished,
and proud:
born in a state of total completion,
it sticks to itself and knows exactly what it wants.

Poetry In Motion© 1996 Marlowe, New York

New York City Transit
In cooperation with Poetry Society of America

I Stop Writing The Poem

TESS GALLAGHER (b.1945)

to fold the clothes. No matter who lives
or who dies, I'm still a woman.
I'll always have plenty to do.
I bring the arms of his shirt
together. Nothing can stop
our tenderness. I'll get back
to the poem. I'll get back to being a
woman. But for now
there's a shirt, a giant shirt
in my hands, and somewhere a small girl
standing next to her mother
watching to see how it's done.

Poetry In Motion© 1996 Marlowe, New York

New York City Transit
In cooperation with Poetry Society of America

POETRY IN MOTION

TRANSIT

A woman I have never seen before
Steps from the darkness of her town-house door
At just that crux of time when she is made
So beautiful that she or time must fade.

What use to claim that as she tugs her gloves
A phantom heraldry of all the loves
Blares from the lintel? That the staggered sun
Forgets, in his confusion, how to run?

Still, nothing changes as her perfect feet
Click down the walk that issues in the street,
Leaving the stations of her body there
As a whip maps the countries of the air.

Richard Wilbur (b. 1921)

Poetry In Motion® 1996 Marlowe, New York

New York City Transit
In cooperation with Poetry Society of America

Thank You, My Dear

Thank you, my dear

You came, and you did
well to come: I needed
you. You have made

love blaze up in
my breast – bless you!
Bless you as often

as the hours have
been endless to me
while you were gone.

Sappho (c 600 B.C.)
Translated by Mary Barnard

Poetry In Motion© 1996 Marlowe, New York

New York City Transit
In cooperation with Poetry Society of America

The Armful

Robert Frost (1874-1963)

For every parcel I stoop down to seize
I lose some other off my arms and knees,
And the whole pile is slipping, bottles, buns–
Extremes too hard to comprehend at once,
Yet nothing I should care to leave behind.
With all I have to hold with, hand and mind
And heart, if need be, I will do my best
To keep their building balanced at my breast.
I crouch down to prevent them as they fall;
Then sit down in the middle of them all.
I had to drop the armful in the road
And try to stack them in a better load.

Poetry In Motion® 1996 Marlowe, New York

New York City Transit
In cooperation with Poetry Society of America

Coal (Excerpt)

Love is a word, another kind of open.
As the diamond comes
into a knot of flame
I am Black
because I come from the earth's inside
take my word for jewel
in the open light.

Audre Lorde (1934-1992)

Poetry In Motion© 1996 Marlowe, New York

New York City Transit
In cooperation with Poetry Society of America

POETRY IN MOTION

for
friendship

For friendship
make a chain that holds,
to be bound to
others, two by two,

a walk, a garland,
handed by hands
that cannot move
unless they hold

Robert Creeley (b.1926)

Poetry In Motion® 1996 Marlowe, New York

New York City Transit
In cooperation with Poetry Society of America

POETRY IN MOTION

Thirteen Ways of Looking at a Blackbird

(Excerpt)

Wallace Stevens (1879-1955)

Among twenty snowy mountains,
The only moving thing
Was the eye of the blackbird....

The blackbird whirled in the autumn winds.
It was a small part of the pantomime....

I do not know which to prefer,
The beauty of inflections
Or the beauty of innuendoes,
The blackbird whistling
Or just after.

Poetry In Motion® 1996 Marlowe, New York

New York City Transit
In cooperation with Poetry Society of America

POETRY IN MOTION

HERMANDAD
Homenaje a Claudio Ptolomeo

Soy hombre: duro poco
y es enorme la noche.
Pero miro hacia arriba:
las estrellas escriben.
Sin entender comprendo:
también soy escritura
y en este mismo instante
alguien me deletrea.

BROTHERHOOD
Homage to Claudius Ptolemy

I am a man: little do I last
and the night is enormous.
But I look up:
the stars write.
Unknowing I understand:
I too am written,
and at this very moment
someone spells me out.

Octavio Paz (b.1914)

Poetry In Motion© 1996 Marlowe, New York

New York City Transit
In cooperation with Poetry Society of America

POETRY IN MOTION

RECUERDO

EXCERPT

We were very tired, we were very merry—
We had gone back and forth all night on the ferry.
And you ate an apple, and I ate a pear,
From a dozen of each we had bought somewhere;
And the sky went wan, and the wind came cold,
And the sun rose dripping, a bucketful of gold.

Edna St. Vincent Millay (1892 - 1950)

Poetry In Motion® 1996 Marlowe, New York

New York City Transit
In cooperation with Poetry Society of America

POETRY IN MOTION

HOPE IS THE THING WITH FEATHERS

"Hope" is the thing with feathers—
That perches in the soul—
And sings the tune without the words—
And never stops—at all—

And sweetest—in the Gale is heard—
And sore must be the storm—
That could abash the little Bird
That kept so many warm—

I've heard it in the chillest land
And on the strangest Sea—
Yet, never, in Extremity,
It asked a crumb—of Me.

—Emily Dickinson (1830-1886)

Poetry In Motion® 1996 Marlowe, New York

New York City Transit
In cooperation with Poetry Society of America

When you are old and grey and full of sleep,
And nodding by the fire, take down this book,
And slowly read, and dream of the soft look
Your eyes had once, and of their shadows deep;

How many loved your moments of glad grace,
And loved your beauty with love false or true,
But one man loved the pilgrim soul in you,
And loved the sorrows of your changing face;

And bending down beside the glowing bars,
Murmur, a little sadly, how Love fled
And paced upon the mountains overhead
And hid his face amid a crowd of stars.

William Butler Yeats (1865-1939)

WHEN YOU ARE OLD

From THE POEMS OF W.B. YEATS: A NEW EDITION,
edited by Richard J Finneran (New York: Macmillan, 1983).
Reprinted with the permission of Simon & Schuster

Poetry In Motion© 1996 Marlowe, New York

New York City Transit
In cooperation with Poetry Society of America

Adolescence - I

In water-heavy nights behind grandmother's porch
We knelt in the tickling grass and whispered:
Linda's face hung before us, pale as a pecan,
And it grew wise as she said:
  "A boy's lips are soft,
  As soft as baby's skin."

The air closed over her words.
A firefly whirred in the air, and in the distance
I could hear streetlamps ping
Into miniature suns
Against a feathery sky.

RITA DOVE (b.1952)

Poetry In Motion© 1996 Marlowe, New York

New York City Transit
In cooperation with Poetry Society of America

Hedgehog

He ambles along like a walking pin cushion,
Stops and curls up like a chestnut burr.
He's not worried because he's so little.
Nobody is going to slap him around.

Chu Chen Po (9th century)
Translated from the Chinese by Kenneth Rexroth

Poetry In Motion® 1996 Marlowe, New York

New York City Transit
In cooperation with Poetry Society of America